DRON LEWIS

THE BEGINNING OF A NEW JOURNEY

publisher logo

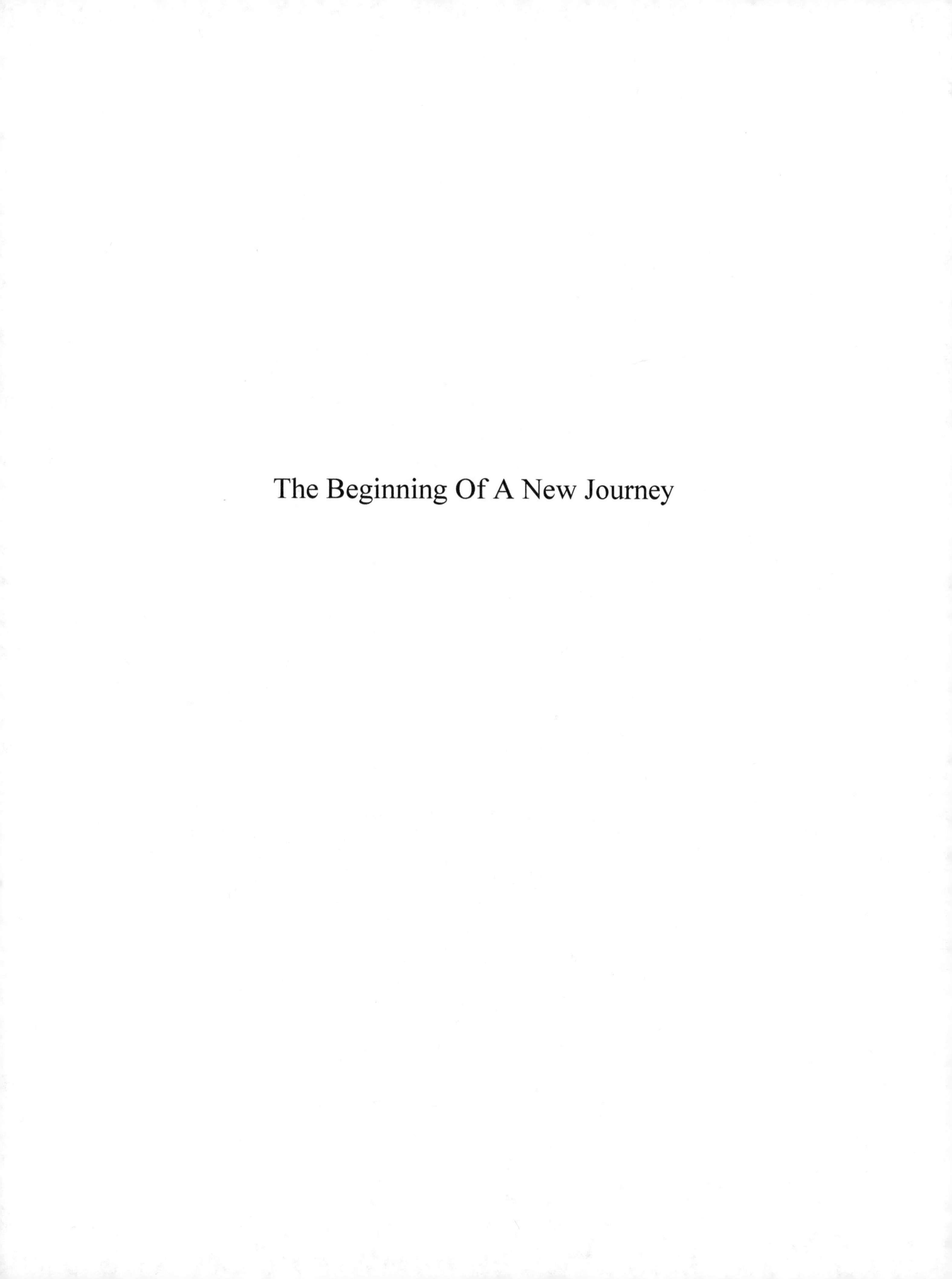

The Beginning Of A New Journey

SET FREE

Remember the hurt and pain through life,
Prejudging the code to a decision,
Acknowledging the wrong rather than the right.

Compounded in your own emotion,
The fear to let it out and flow.
Tough love calls within the flesh,
But Evil lurks on the soul.

Clouded in the storming darkness,
Answering to the wicked judgment.
Material things in your line of sight
What makes you any different.

Stuck in between love and hate,
Through the days with no peace
A mind set on giving it up, A heart filled with balls of grief.

The trembling of your bones,
Shoulders weighing on your feet.

You try to go step by step,

But your body feels so weak.

Someone calls out in a loud voice,

Confused on what to do next.

See nothing in complete darkness,

But receive a feeling in your chest.

A light shine on your life,

As if putting you in a spot.

Healing every inch of a scar,

Only bringing a moment of shock.

Comfort runs through the veins,

Peace flows within the heart.

Eyes clear of deceitful mist,

Now you shine in the dark.

Walking with such a change,

Strength on top of your feet.

Smile for the days are brighter,

Tears of joy run down your cheeks.

My soul now has coverage,

An Experience of heavens treat.

The chains have been broken,

What a wonderful feeling to finally be "SET FREE".

A CHOICE TO MAKE

Living in a corrupted generation, Blind following the Blind not knowing who is really leading the nation. Standing side by side tearing each other down trying to beat each other to greatness but Jesus is the only way we make it so who are you living for?

It's going to be an unexpected time when the sky will be red as blood, many claim to have it understood but follow their own mind as if they could survive on their own strength. Walking to impress the people, shouting the names that are corrupted by the devil like are you willing to take your foot off the peddle, make a U turn to start a new level.

Jesus is calling us, why put up a fuss when you hear gospel being preached to all nations if its Jesus you trust. We all have a choice to make, Seeking Jesus is the key, there is no mistake, stop worrying about who will support you or take this walk with you because everybody will be judged with their own case so let's focus. Jesus will put individuals in your life who are meant to be, pull out those who are a distraction, they can never build up to your satisfaction even if they are apart of the family tree.

We must love him more than anything, Yes God is the creator of everything, Jesus died so we can have many days and forgive the sins that we commit in many ways, so go to Christ and pray, acknowledge him and his holy name. A new heaven and a new earth will be arranged when this world is destroyed by fire, Striving to go higher to be with Christ and his grace we must truly desire, the Word Of God truly inspires the souls of the world that the devil tries to rewire, we must resist his evil.

Time is running short like it is being snatched, at the end there will be no time to worry about if the earth was flat, there is no catch, He wants a relationship with us but don't live your life putting him to the test. Love Christ more than yourself, that's also true, walk with faith and trust you won't be lead to be a fool, listen to the messages God is sending, he is guiding you through, so the question is will you choose Jesus Christ or will you choose you?

ONE MILE LONGER

Such a world to fulfill a purpose,

Short cut to the bottom,

A long way to the surface,

Broken confidence trying to make it perfect,

Is there even a point to see if it's worth it.

One way or another it must be reached,

So many obstacles stopping at your feet,

But remember why you started this streak,

Its time to take it One Mile Longer.

Failure was never an option,

Yet it happens time and time again,

Knocking hard on the door of success,

Wondering why it won't let you in.

Pray for strength and take your mark,

Push through leaving a positive spark,

You have made it a long way from the start,

Let's take it One Mile Longer.

Acknowledge he who gives you your days,

The chances that are given to make your way,

As you stand to run another race,

Close your eyes and let your heart be filled with grace.

From the smallest mustard seed,

To the tallest olive tree,

The process of growth is the key,

Its time to take it One Mile Longer.

Mistakes will be made even in a walk,

Fly high like an eagle and have eyes like a hawk,

Actions speak louder so there is no need to talk,

Be wise and let your peace be locked.

Honor to the most high, He is with you so continue to try.

You might fall short and urge to cry,

But with Jesus everything is possible,

Pick up your cross and take it One Mile Longer.

A THIN ROAD TO PEACE

What is such a Feeling, Is it a treasure of gold.

Can it be found underneath the earth,

Does it have secrets that it may hold.

It is time to start a search, let nothing get in the way.

But what if it's a dead end, could it just be another fantasy play.

So much of worldly desires, they must be reached today,

The mind being told a lie, like money can make a smile stay.

Only a few people find it, In such a world of struggle.

Focus on the task at hand, let the lord have a rebuttal.

Walk towards the brightest light, Bring forth a sigh of relief,

But Enemies will rock the ground, Shifting the balance under your feet.

Crumbling like the side of a cliff, Most of the way disappears.

Yet the Hand of Christ reaches out to you,

Stretch your arms out and make your way near. Conquer what is meant to be, Heavens rejoices for an angels speech.

For when that time comes, there will be peace for all eternity.

Struggle for a lifetime has corrupted a strong heart, the weight of a once faithful being begins to heavy, dragging the feet of an extraordinary mind filled with a great vision but what more can I do?

Strictly thriving to live for the one and only, focus on completing the mission set before me, while surrounded by the things of life reminding the heart of a guilty past.

The feeling of failing every test that comes between now and what is to come but only if it was simple, NO! for even this life is not for a simple mind. You know what is within you.

Carrying a gift that no one can snatch out of your grasp. Stumbling and Fumbling but keep your balance, don't you dare give up. Future times are uncertain yet the present is a gift to all.

Remember what you are called to do going step by step, its okay to take it slow. A light is shining on your life guiding you through your purpose.

Remember who supports you above all things of world and stay encouraged. Cherish the ups and downs for when that glorious day comes, there will be on lookers as the on above presents a "Gifted Soul".

When I pray, I pray that the people of the nations come to the knowledge of truth. I pray that faith grows in individuals that simply struggles to have a place to stay. I pray the wars of the world come to have a place in the soldier's hearts to end in peace so that children can make it home safe. Yet we are in the last days but I know god still hears me when I pray.

Always a problem in these days, prices going up like money grow on trees as people say. What specific narrative can change the fact we the people make it hard to live today but complain about worldly trauma that we put into play. When I pray, I pray that the young people of this generation come to realization that we do not need to follow the way of the wicked. I pray that the children exposed to violence finds someone bold enough to show them the right direction. I pray that parents that stop being so young to the point they are close in age with their child. Yet we are in the last days, I know god still hears me when I pray.

As we break into the new year and possibly many years to come, we must focus on the task at hand that the creator of this world and all generations has put before us. These days and nights are a battle within the mind as if we need to rush, but still thank God for the struggles and the blessings in this life he has gave all of us. And as the greatest return has yet to come, I pray that we grow in a relationship so strong in connection even on the darkest planet, the way out will be clear.

As Martin Luther King had a dream, I pray that all walks of life come together to bow down and praise the hole one who is drawing near. There is no need to fear, for peace is coming to those who believe in the Almighty Son of God whose presence is already here. Though we are in the final days, I know God still hears me when I pray.

There is an unimaginable place that awaits to be opened and there is a Great God whom is preparing a return for his people but am I prepared?

Living like many believing in the mind that if he could save us at this very moment from this evil world. Yet there is a voice calling out to me telling me to be patient my child for your heart is not ready. I have still much to get done before the great coming.

We are all set for a purpose even so trials and tribulations may clous our judgment. As so long I walk this earth facing challenges of every level of difficulty, I shall follow my lord and savior until he calls me home.

If many enemies stand in my future's way, prepare me to walk through with a loving and pure heart.

When I get pushed down, give me the strength to stand tall for the glory of your name. Fill me with the holy spirit and work within me the will of the father.

Let faith grow stronger in the savior so that no matter how many times I fall, I know he hears me when I call, even when everything is wrong, I shall continue to follow my lord and savior until he calls me home.

When the sun shines in the morning, my mind shall cling to the purpose that God is preparing me for. No Darkness will ever blind my path as my savior promised.

To hear well done thy good and faithful servant, thy will be done on earth as it is in heaven forever more until he calls me home.

SAVE ME

O Lord, why do I feel forsaken? Could anyone carry such a burden on their shoulders? To feel stuck to the gravitational pull of darkness.

Inside the thoughts of a constant overthinking mind where demons like to swing around the imagination of a struggling heart.

Battles within a war left and right, to have to fight for a space of peace yet I fall to the flesh that is weak while trying to seek a way out.

O Lord, please save me from the chains that are holding me down. Save me from the wolfs that are attacking your lost sheep.

I know your sacrifice was not in vain for a promise made that even in shallow grave your light is everlasting, but I'm blinded and ask for your guidance.

Take my hand and pull me out of what feels like oil and water. As I cry out your name O Lord I say please save me.

What is Faith?

Faith is confidence in what is to come. Not a feeling or emotion but a personal decision to make within your heart.

Many things might not always go your way no matter how hard you work. Test of your faith will always come about when you are getting closer to the purpose that God has given you.

As the lord our god leads us, let not our hearts grow weary in times of trouble. But why should we face trouble throughout the walk of life?

God didn't promise a perfect life for mankind on the earth for that is already prepared for us but many have no clue. By Faith, the works of God will bestow great blessings on those who believe and love God.

While all things were made perfect yet destroyed by us, it was by faith and love that God sent his only begotten son to die on the cross for our sins.

Live by Faith with all your heart and trust in the lord, for faith is the way to pleasing God.

Working to the point confidence won't even be cracked when the plan starts to fall apart.

Like a stream of water flowing with the land guiding it to the open ocean, by faith we trust in the lord that he will continue to guide his people to the kingdom of God.

Dear God, I am thankful for everything you have done for me,

I was stuck in a demon cage until you finally set me free.

I remember so long ago when I couldn't sleep at night,

But now when I dream, I believe this is what peace feels like.

The struggle in every relationship just felt like one big consequence,

Yet ever since you saved me now I know what true love is.

Each day I will fall to sin never thinking how bad the path was,

Took my hand and pulled me away even when I was giving up.

There was no love on my heart, thought that
I had lost the war,

Then you laid your hand on my life now I
know who I'm living for.

I pray that you remember me on the day of
your great return,

And after I will praise your name forever and
ever more.

So I say Dear God, I'm thankful for every-
thing you have done for me,

I was stuck in a demon cage until you finally
set me free.

It is written " So now Faith, Hope, and Love abide these three but The Greatest of those is Love." 1 Corinthians 13:13

Who can really understand the deeds of love or what it comes with? Are we supposed to do everything in every way for love?

Surely, we must love with a pure heart and not expect things in return. But out of all things done in love, What is The Greatest Love?

Someone can bring harm or verbal negativity to break a heart and can be forgiven. We can do something to ourselves and go on with life loving ourselves without any guilt. But No Evil can be done in love yet we find that as the best option if it is one.

For "Greater love has no one than this to lay down one's life for one's friend." John 15:13. So I say The Greatest Love is Jesus Christ himself who gave his life for all humanity without any regret.

So that we may have a way to eternal peace, joy, and happiness living in harmony with one another. Jesus Christ chose us over himself and lived again to tell the story and rather believed or not, Jesus Christ is The Greatest Love.

GOODNESS OF THE FRUIT

Who bears such a good thing in which we must live by. The spread of peace and not evil that leaves such division in the world.

Yeah, for many have their own beliefs in this temporary reality but who truly bears the goodness of the fruit to which is fueled through the Holy Spirit.

Oh how life would be if many were to try it, the better character that will come into play. Out with the old and in with the new heart and soul a good fruitful spirit to be shared across the globe.

But yet we can only sense the actual bad fruit the eyes can see but not the ones within us. How corrupted we all really are lost in our minds of evil.

In the darkness of the world where no one seeks the light of freedom. For only those who have the goodness of the fruit through the spirit are truly free.

The feeling to not carry the weight of rotten emotion and live in harmony bringing peace and positivity everywhere you go. We must ask ourselves this question, is your fruit corrupted?

A CROWN TO RECEIVE

By day and by night trouble is near,

Dark all around me, growing my fear,

If only there was something to make every-
thing clear,

I know in my heart this life is worth more
than what it bears.

Yes indeed I hear a voice say, trust in me
and you won't be lead astray.

I hear your cries when you pray everyday,

so continue to keep your faith as your re-
ward awaits your stay.

Walk and walk and walk your life full of joy
and peace, Even with no strength in your feet.

Never give up walking for me even if you have to take a seat, then time will come to pass and your crown you shall receive.

No matter how tough life gets prayer is the answer to everything. Otherwise where would we be trusting our own minds that would most likely leave us confused.

How would we know how to handle any situations without the answers from our creator? Yeah, sometimes we won't understand but even Jesus said later we will.

For money can't solve every problem even if you have enough yet it just brings more. Can search the internet in many ways but it can't teach us how to pray. Matthew 6: 9-13

Prayer connects us through the holy spirit in which God speaks to us. It might feel sometimes that God is not listening but he is with us every step of the way.

We will begin to realize just how peaceful prayer is, I mean… it sure beats arguing and misunderstanding.

Let it become a lifestyle to pray to the most holy one because everyday he is showering his blessings onto the lives of you and I.

OH, If Things got easier each day, every battle that ever came my way. If I looked up and it never stormed and took away the light, even when I look down and the green on the grass was always in sight.

Never receiving a bad call and things always staying in place, I could just smile and say I just won another race. But I know in reality that is not how this life goes. I will fall or trip my toes.

Yet the lord is the reason that I grow so I praise him everywhere I go. Even when a mountain is in my way, my strength could never move it away, but he strengthens me through all things, so I praise him every day.

From the dark and lonely nights to the gloomy and rainy storms I will always trust him and my faith shall never be torn. During the wars across the world and enemies that try to take a stand, Jesus is Lord so I praise him until he returns again.

We all have a purpose set before us by our creator,

Different Gifts to be used in the most ex-tradentary ways,

You might think sometimes what the point of this life is really,

Yeah, I have to… but wait do you hear that?

That voice above the clouds coming from the mouth of him who watches over us.

Such a strong vocal, isn't it? And he is speaking to you and I.

You have a gift inside of you that can change your life and many others.

He wants to use you for the greater of his will.

Allow him to take you on a journey of a life-time where greater things await.

There is a calling for you my friend, pick it up and watch your life change Forever. Only he can make you into the person you truly are.

We all have challenges and battles we have lost.

It will get hard to the point you think about giving up.

But even after hardships there is victory, so trust in the lord because a change is coming.

Look to the sky but the sun will not always shine.

Yet even in the storm you are guided through it by the spirit.

Let's focus on the goal that he has set before us.

Not everything will come as easy as it seems.

But trust in the lord for a change is coming.

You feel like you're just going in circles.

You trip even though there is nothing under your feet.

There is a race to be won so don't you dare quit.

Take it a day at a time and allow him to guide you.

You are getting close so trust in the lord because a change is coming.

You will cry lonely nights,

As if you lost the fight,

But everything will be alright,

There is Joy Coming in the Morning.

You will have stressful days,

Yet the lord still sends us on our way,

This is why we still give him praise,

Because There is Joy Coming in the Morn-
ing.

You try to take it an extra mile,

Change hasn't come in quite a while,

But even knowing that in your mind you still
smile,

Why is That?

"THERE IS JOY COMING IN THE MORN-ING"

I know this life is not forever but to be with you always is hard to let go.

All of the great moments we had with one another just makes it hard to believe you gone.

We can be apart for so long and reunite and still have that great connection.

The Unforgettable times you made me laugh sometimes I ask myself why would such a pure heart be taken away?

If you could just step out and take your moment of shine one more time but I don't even know if that would enough.

A True Angel of God you were, and I believe you have gained your wings.

So, Fly high my friend for I know this is not goodbye. You will always be in my heart.

Tears of Joy come down my eyes for I know you are eternally at peace.

Until Next Time, farewell my friend as we celebrate your legacy and honor your life.

"In Loving Memory Of Eric Ozan"

There is a lot of evil in this world around every corner. You can avoid it, but it always finds a way to you no matter what.

It can even be in your own household which I believe is the worst. But God said there will be such things happening within.

Yeah, it hurts to see your own blood do something evil against you. Yet God only needs one for great works in a family.

When we go out into the outside world, we must live in harmony and peace with one another. That also needs to be within the family as well.

No matter what is done, the holy spirit within you will help with stand anything the enemy throws at you even in your family.

As Long as you continue to allow the holy spirit to work your mind, heart, and soul as you believed.

In due time, God would have reached the hearts of your bloodline through your spiritually gifted soul.

Then you will see " A Saved Family" in Christ who all will be remembered in the Kingdom of God.

I say Glory to the Father,

Because he deserves the praise,

He led me to my purpose,

And He took away my pain.

I learned to let go of my past,

My eyes were full of rain,

But then he answered my call,

Now I am forever saved.

So I say Glory to the Father,

Because he deserves the praise,

He led me to my purpose,

And he took away my pain.

My heart can now love again,

Set Free from all my sins,

For when I am in trouble,

I know that I can call on him.

From the morning sunshine,

To the shine of the moonlight,

I learned to forgive my enemies,

That is better than a sacrifice.

So I say Glory to the Father,

Because he deserves the praise,

When I look up to a cloudy sky,I know that I
am saved.

You feel convicted within yourself as if right is nowhere to be found.

But you call on the Almighty God as your knees start to hit the ground.

Not knowing what to pray for or at least how to get it off your chest.

You just wish that it would be over and all be laid to rest.

Something just continues to pull you back or do you turn the other way.

Worry builds up in your heart, but you know that is must not stay.

Push forward toward the purpose God set before you, there are many who need you too.

But your past still weighs on you, you believe you have failed him so many times.

Why would he trust me again or even hear my cry.

Yet you pray and pray trusting he will guide you and relieve you of your pride.

What if I am tempted and fall into such a sin another time? Would it just be easier to just rewind?

If that were true, many if not all would choose that path but that would not change the future mistakes.

He is the forgiver of all sin so one prayer is all it takes.

Don't let this define you but his spirit within your heart, look up and follow his light for you are called to be set apart.

You're going to slip, and you are going to fall but you keep going through the wind.

Because A Saint Is Nothing But A Sinner, to fall and get back again.

You are going through a lot right now as if the pain is never fading.

It is hard to imagine if you will make it out but you're still standing.

You cry and cry wondering why things are really going bad.

As If your emotions don't know rather to be happy or rather to be sad, and you let it all out all at once to show a broken heart.

When are all the great things finally going to start?

But there is a reason why you're walking and still have breathe.

There is a reason why you still have a little life in you left.

Just look up to the sky and close your eyes and remember why your strength in there.

Its God's Work in the atmosphere of where you stand.

He is the reason why we can thrive through-out all the land.

Don't let the failures define who you are in his name.

Let him create a great work in you because there are blessings for you to claim.

Then when things start to finally go in your life, you can just say "Thank God".

Because it is God's Work why we all have a place to serve him.

So be encouraged and know that he is not done with you yet.

These are not our battles that we fight so be still and take a breathe.

If you are feeling down, just say a prayer and he will hear your voice.

He will wipe your tears and block out all the noise and bring you joy.

See by God's Work there is a gift stored inside of you and is waiting to be embraced.

Just let him move his hand across your life and remarkable things will come your way and you will see by God's Work, you were able to finish the race.

Now I woke up this morning and I started on my way.

Don't know what this day might bring but I am walking with my faith.

Yes, I might even fall or maybe not reach a Goal.

Will even see my share of trouble that will try to knock me real low.

But out of all the things that will attack my heart.

I just look up to my savior and say well this is the start of Another Day's Journey walking with you my friend.

I will always continue to trust in you forever
until the end.

Its Another Day's Journey with strength un-
der my feet.

Walking with my head held high knowing
you are all I need.

Even when I start to have my share of loneli-
ness like if that is ever true.

I know if I stayed that way I would be a fool
because you are with me and I trust you.

Things won't always go my way but I still go
down and pray.

You are the only one who makes me smile
and brings me joy every day.

When trouble comes my way on each of my
days, I just look up to my savior and say that

this is the start of Another Day's Journey
walking with you my friend.

I will always continue to trust in you forever
until the end.

Its Another Day's Journey with strength un-
der my feet.

Walking with my head held high knowing
that you are all I need.

ANGEL WINGS

Time is running out to the end my trial.

The will be no tears and no pain in the end and the spirit that is within me, I pray that you remember me.

Because Jesus you are the reason I smile even when I'm hurt under the weather.

And when I am falling apart, I know that you are putting me back together.

So When I see your face and able to hold you tight, I will thank you for saving my life.

The day I receive my angel wings and conquer my dream to serve you at your heavenly feet.

Nothing else can compare to the power that you have and the life that always bring to me.

Even when I am confused about some things, you direct where you want me to.

Help me not to worry and always trust in you even when we are taking it slow because I know…

As long as I make it to you in the end is when I will truly win.

No more wars and evil surrounding my life ever again.

All the love and the joy that will be shown on that day as I will be giving you praise.

The day I receive my angel wings and conquer my dream to serve you at your heavenly feet.

To look to the sky and see your great return
is the greatest thing I will ever see.

The day I receive my Angel Wings.

____

OH how my heart was seeking love and peace yet it was so hard to find.

I was doing not such great things, looking at all the wrong places at one time.

It just felt like a rush of pain and confusion as the days came to a close.

But who would have thought you would be the greatest person I would have ever known.

Oh My lord how time slowed down when we met and I could finally take a breathe.

The search had finally came to an end how the pain disappeared from my chest.

You guided me through so many situations and blessed me in so many ways.

You took my hand and promised that you will always stay.

Whenever I would call, you would answer when I pray.

I don't like stumbling or making any mistake against you.

But how your generous mercy gave me courage to stay calm and cool.

You have shown me so many things some-times my mind can't keep track of.

Yet I know when I trust you, your light will shine on my life like a dove.

Oh My lord how time slowed down when we met and I could finally take a breath.

Now I know what true love is and who really knows me best.

When I used to wake up, I had hate on my mind and it was never going to go away.

Thought I really knew people but it wasn't true so I started acting like a fool but then your angels touched me.

Could never talk about the things that were hurting me but when you came around, it was easy to.

I know I had a lot of lows when you made me yours then you touched my heart now I feel alive.

Thought I was alone then I made it to my peace, now turning over a new leaf and now I am chasing a new dream, and it all because you "Jesus Christ" called my name.

Now He is changing my ways and I am living for the best each and every day.

Praising his name as he is changing my ways and bringing me peace every time I pray.

And I will never be alone again because he is the only friend that remains true.

His is the only way that I will make it out of every situation that comes my way.

So I trust him and never take it into my own hands because trusting myself will only lead me astray again. Now I am slow to speak and quick to listen.

As He is changing my ways, I will continue to grow closer to him with no delay.

Even if I fall, I know that I will be okay because Jesus is with me every step of the way.

Most days will have more trouble than you
can probably handle.

Life is filled with many doors, but you con-
tinue to open the wrong one.

It gets hard but through it all there is one
place that is waiting just to open up for us.

So when you think you had enough but then
the sun starts coming up, and you remember
in your heart.

There is a Heavenly place for us where
there is joy and peace when we are finally
free.

The pain is completely gone so you will
never feel weak.

Many angels singing and dancing and children laughing never a tear in sight.

Knowing what the father has prepared for us just makes you feel alright.

Get your confidence up and strengthen your faith and smile through it all.

Because the day is coming when the doors will open, and that smile will never go away.

It's A Heavenly Place for us where there is joy and peace when we are finally Free.

Tears are dry from your eyes and never return again, So whenever you start to feel down, just remember this my friend.

Something greater is coming in time and it will all be worth it in the end.

Everything is messing up though you try and try again.

You try and look for help but no one is lending a helping hand.

Tears start to fall down your eyes like a river down a stream.

You have it in your mind that you just wanna scream.

But even through the pain, just look how far you came and the reason your standing on your feet.

It is he within you that strengthens you and gives you what you need so just Learn to trust Him.

He is the reason we get through our days, He even said such things will happen but that don't mean take your smile away.

Keep on praying and lift up your hands even when the pain continues to grow.

That voice tells you to give it up but there is something you should know.

Learn to trust Him, no matter how weak you get. He is a healer and will deliver you to be a part of his perfect plan.

You ways are never the best and life will put you the test, then when you call on him, he will bless you with victory.

So Learn to trust Him.

The Sun starts to get really low most of this life.

Seems like darkness clouds your mind throughout the night.

Worried about what the next day may possibly bring.

You don't know if you are ready to continue this walk of suffering.

Don't take it into your own hands for your plan is never right.

Remember He that is way ahead of your fight.

Keep Praying that things will work in your favor.

Even when it seems nothing is going to change now or later.

Keep Praying until something happens in your season of waiting.

You may suffer in this time as if God does not hear what you are saying.

But stay encouraged and set your chin up to the most high.

So when your life turns to greater blessings, you will know that he is always on time.

Dark days are among us but not forever in this life.

They will come unexpectedly just when everything is going alright.

There will be times when emotion will start to overflow and tears will start to fall.

Many will feel repeated as time continues to move along.

But even in the night as you walk under the sky, the stars still shine.

So be faithful in the day that comes next that God gifted us with his light.

Because greater is the light and no darkness shall overcome it.

And your days will be brighter always for-
ever in the end.

Thorns in the ground leaving many scars on my feet.

So much pain locked in my heart and it seems I can't find the key.

Wake up in the morning wondering how I am going to feed my soul.

Many voices in my head and they whisper in my ear that I should go ahead and let go.

Didn't think I was going to make it as I was waiting on a change.

But at the time when there was no hope I finally made it through the rain.

It was all by the Grace of God and I will never have to worry again.

No matter what happens in the future, I
know I will be able to win.

Saved by the Grace of God, whenever I fall,
I can overcome it.

The devil thought he had me then I fell on
my knees and prayed to my savior.

Now when things are falling down or I fall
short to a sin.

My God is a prayer away because I know I
am Saved by his Grace.

"Clear your mind"

Imagine floating in the sky with a slow breeze brushing against your face.

To be above the trouble of the world with no harm to come your way.

Surrounded in the presence of God as you close your eyes and feel his peace.

Seeing all that he created without a worry of the enemy.

Stretch out your arms and be as free as you will ever be.

Imagine yourself on a holy cloud moving freely with the angels of God.

Smiling as all the trouble and pain were never there.

That is Gods blessing to you when you go to him in prayer.

Everything will be okay as it is all in gods hands.

So continue to believe in his name until we see him again.

The battles that I face are getting overwhelm-
ing.

Don't know what the enemy into tomorrow
might bring.

I fall on my knees and shout as I start pray-
ing.

My lord I know you hear me when I call on
your name.

I am asking that you please retore my soul
in these troubled days.

Let your light shine on this road because I
know you are the only way.

I know you promised me that you were here
to stay.

So I know when I call your name everything will be okay.

My lord please Restore My Soul for the enemy is roaming throughout the land.

Because I know without your protection I cannot stand.

Give me strength to walk the narrow road according to your will.

For all is for your glory through my faith as I stop and be still.

There are many cracks in the ground that I tripped and fell.

It feels like the pain is increasing and it's not hard to tell.

The beating of my heart is slowing down and that's not going well.

So I ask that you hear me as I say this prayer.

My lord please Restore my Soul as this life goes on.

No matter what is in the air, correct me if I even breathe wrong.

Bring me through the trials that the enemy may use to bring me down.

Even when I'm lost, guide my heart to where I will always be found.

Your life is full of ups and downs and you are running out of luck.

Bills are piling up and it just keeps getting tough.

Looking at the blessings that are just passing by your life.

Then you start to question what is it your not doing right.

The earth keeps spinning but nothing seems to move.

Its in your mind to give up like you have nothing else to lose.

But there is something that you still haven't tried.

Call on the God who hears you when you cry.

He will take away your pain and change your soul around.

Then you will be surprised when your feet start to get off the ground.

Your days are looking up and there is no longer a frown.

He laid his hand on your life, brought out your heart, you are all filled with Joy and Now you have a reason to smile.

You may feel alone right now like there is no one to save the day.

You walk around seeking for help but there is no one to lead the way.

Your heart feels so empty from life that not even family can fill the void.

Dreams are fading and you don't want to go through with it anymore.

But there is somebody who will make it better.

Somebody looking to make your days brighter.

Somebody who will bring that love and hope toward your heart.

Let me tell you about Jesus Christ.

Call His name and he will straighten all your paths.

Surrender your life and he will bring you first from the last.

I am talking about somebody who will bring your soul peace as you rest.

When the trials come on the darkest days, he will guide you out always and he is just waiting for you to take his hand.

Let him elevate your mind to shine bright amongst a crowd for his glory.

Because at the end of the journey, you will see it was worth it to let Jesus write your story.

Yes, he is somebody who will change your life.

He is somebody who will wash your tears out of your eyes.

Ease your pain and open up those gates in your heart and he is waiting for you to let him in.

He gave his life for us so why wouldn't you trust him.

He wants to know you and you come to know him.

Let him take your dreams and make them greater.

His name is Jesus Christ, He is and always will be our savior.

There are many things of the world the enemy
uses to knock you off your way.

The sun burns steaming hot that you won-
der if you will even survive the day.

Winter snow now may fall on your head and
build up to your knees as you walk, just an-
other thing increasing your pain.

Follow Jesus Anyway

Bad news seems to come into both ears
constantly building up stress.

You pray everyday and everynight for heal-
ing in your chest.

But we have to understand that everyday of
life will always be a test.

So Follow Jesus Anyway

Even if you have to stop and take a seat.

Dust off your shoulders and clean the mud
from under your feet.

You may be tired and feel that the journey
may have you beat.

Follow Jesus Anyway

This long narrow road may feel to be lonely
at times.

Though many are called, even the enemy is
lurking in the line.

But how do you know that all of this is really
worth the time?

Follow Jesus Anyway

When you reach the end of this road he lead you to.

You would think that everything was to good to be true.

Looking at what you accomplished and all the trials that you believed you wouldn't make it through.

Now you are blessed with treasure falling on your life because you believed and Followed Jesus Anyway.

Many storms become so strong even when
it is just the rain.

I close my eyes to try and tune out what's
causing the pain.

I am running trying to clear my mind as the
winds blow free.

The trials come in and seem to not come out
and it just feels like an Eternity.

But Lord I'll be still and trust in your name.

My mind could never take on the thoughts of
giving up alone in any way.

So as I open my eyes and look to the sky
where the clouds slowly move.

Many voices play in my head and I pray that
one voice is you.

But I'll be still and trust in your name.

Even when goals fall apart and become out
of reach.

When there is a crack in the ship of peace
and it all begins to sink.

As the enemy tries to attack in my dreams
as I sleep.

I will trust you will always be there to cover
me.

Like the waves that push against the shore
of the land.

Life will knock me down as I strive to follow
the plan.

Enemies draw near to me, always trying to get close enough to stick.

Yet I know praying that you will guard my heart will always do the trick.

So I'll be Still and trust in your name.

Because you are all I need for the rest of my days.